Sew Gifty

Sew Gifty

Fun Accessories, Décor Accents, Baby Gifts, and Other Perfect Presents

JANIS BULLIS

Creative Publishing international

Chanhassen, MN

ACKNOWLEDGMENTS

For thread and zippers:
Coats and Clark
PO Box 12229
Greenville SC 29612
(800) 648-1479
www.coatsandclark.com

For interfacing, stabilizers and fusibles:
Pellon® Consumer Products
4720-A Stone Drive
Tucker, GA 30084
(800) 223-5275
www.pellonideas.com

For ribbon and trimming:
Wrights®
PO Box 398
West Warren, MA 01092
(800) 660-0415
www.wrights.com

For fabric:
Oilcloth International, Inc.
134 N. Avenue 61, Bldg. 101
Los Angeles, CA 90042
(323) 334-3967
www.oilcloth.com

**Creative Publishing
international**

Copyright 2006
Creative Publishing international
18705 Lake Drive East
Chanhassen, Minnesota 55317
1-800-328-3895
www.creativepub.com
All rights reserved

President/CEO: Ken Fund
Executive Editor: Alison Brown Cerier
Executive Managing Editor: Barbara Harold
Senior Editor: Linda Neubauer
Photo Stylist: Joanne Wawra
Creative Director: Brad Springer
Photo Art Director: Tim Himsel
Photographer: Steve Galvin
Production Manager: Laura Hokkanen
Cover Design: Dania Davey
Interior Design: Lois Stanfield
Illustration: Deborah Pierce

Library of Congress Cataloging-in-Publication Data

Bullis, Janis.
  Sew Gifty : Fun Accessories, Décor Accents, Baby Gifts, and
Other Perfect Presents / JanisBullis.
      p. cm.
ISBN-13: 978-1-58923-273-0 (soft cover)
  ISBN-10: 1-58923-273-9 (soft cover)
  1. Needlework--Patterns. 2. Fancy work. I. Title.
TT751.B95 2006
  746--dc22   2006006264

Printed in China:
10 9 8 7 6 5 4 3 2 1

CONTENTS

SPECIAL GIFTS **6**

Silk Beauty Bag **8**

Knitter's Roll **12**

Beach Babe Tote **16**

Two-Story Tote **20**

Luxury Shoe Bags **24**

First-Place Stadium Cushion **28**

Custom Necktie **32**

Friendly Elephant Bib **36**

Curly Soft Bear **40**

Puppy-Dog Hat and Scarf **44**

Charmed Socks **48**

Ballerina Tutu **50**

My Own Lunch Bag **54**

Dressy Guest Towels **58**

Deluxe Linen Napkins **60**

Retro Kitchen Placemats and Napkins **64**

Autumn Leaves Runner **66**

Beaded Table Scarf **68**

Special Year Ornament **70**

Sheer Gift Bags **74**

Fancy Fabric Boxes **78**

PATTERNS **82**

SPECIAL GIFTS

Sewing is a cure for the common gift. In one evening, you can create a gift that is clever, personal, unique, and meaningful. You give a special gift, and at the same time, you give yourself a chance to express your creative side!

So get ready to enjoy yourself as you choose from a wide variety of wonderful, easy-to-sew gifts perfect for everybody on your list. You will find in this collection presents for women, men, babies, and children. There are gifts for every season, for holidays, for birthdays, for your host, for a wedding couple, and for other events and occasions.

Each of the projects is designed to be deluxe, clever, and out of the ordinary—like something you might find in a boutique, only made with your clever touches and probably at less cost. Begin with a beautiful fabric. Most of the projects do not require much fabric, so you can afford a silk or imitation suede or other special fabric. Personalize the project with choices of trims or by adding a press-on monogram.

For each project, you will have step-by-step instructions with photographs. The patterns are at the back of the book. The sewing will be easy, even if you are a beginner.

Finally, a thank-you to my family and friends for celebrating birthdays, weddings, and the birth of new babies, providing me with opportunities to make them gifts. It was my pleasure!

Janis Bullis

JANIS BULLIS has been a sewing writer, designer, and consultant for more than twenty-five years, working with book, magazine, and pattern publishers as well as craft and textile manufacturers. Janis has contributed to more than a hundred how-to publications on topics ranging from bridal accessories to holiday decorating. Her goal is to help people enjoy the many benefits and rewards of creative sewing.

Janis lives in a suburb of New York City with her husband, Jack, and sewing room companion, Penny, a chocolate Labrador.

SILK BEAUTY BAG

MATERIALS

Copy machine or graph paper for enlarging pattern

Paper and pencil for drawing pattern

Carpenter's square or T-square ruler

5/8 yd. (0.6 m) print fabric, 44" (112 cm) wide

1/2 yd. (0.5 m) solid fabric, 44" (112 cm) wide

5/8 yd. (0.6 m) lightweight transparent vinyl

Lightweight quilt batting, 15" × 17" (38 × 43 cm)

Fabric marking pen or pencil

3/4 yd. (0.7 m) double-fold bias tape

Thread

18" (46 cm) zipper

Hand-sewing needle

Seam ripper

1/4 yd. (0.25 m) lightweight fusible interfacing

Bodkin or tube turner

Pretty on the outside but practical on the inside, this makeup bag will please a woman who loves to travel. The easy-clean vinyl lining has six pockets to hold cosmetics (or jewelry). The full-length zipper closure allows the bag to open wide, and the bag is lightly padded to protect what's inside. You can dress up the bag with an embroidered silk, or choose a washable fabric for durability.

FINISHED SIZE: 11¹/₂" WIDE × 6" TALL × 2" DEEP (29.3 × 15 × 5 CM)

I Enlarge the patterns for the outer bag/lining and pockets on page 82, and cut them out. Draw three patterns using paper, pencil, and a carpenter's square or T-square ruler:

Boxing strip: 3" × 21" (7.5 × 53.5 cm)

Handle: 2" × 10" (5 × 25.5 cm)

Handle interfacing: 9½" × 1" (24.3 × 2.5 cm).

These patterns and dimensions include ½" (1.3 cm) seam allowances.

2 Cut one outer bag and two boxing strips from the print fabric. Cut one bag lining and four handles from the solid fabric. Cut one bag lining and one pocket piece from the vinyl. Cut one bag body from the batting. Cut two handle interfacing pieces. Transfer the pocket stitching lines and bottom stitching lines to the solid lining piece. Transfer the handle placement marks to the outer bag.

3 Wrap double-fold bias tape over each of the two straight edges of the vinyl pocket piece and stitch in place. Place the vinyl pocket piece over the vinyl lining piece, using the pattern as a guide. Place the vinyl pieces over the right side of the solid lining piece. Stitch through all three layers along the pocket stitching lines.

4 Place the batting over the wrong side of the outer bag. Baste the two layers together ¼" (6 mm) from the edge.

5 Press one boxing strip in half to mark the center; unfold. Mark a point on the fold 1½" (3.8 cm) from each end. Pin the boxing strips right sides together. Stitch from the ends to the marks, backstitching at the marks. Machine-baste down the center between marks. Fold each boxing strip wrong sides together so the right sides face out on both sides and the basted seam is down the center. Press.

6 Center the zipper, right side down, over the basted part of the boxing strip seam. Hand-baste the zipper in place.

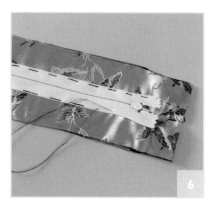

7 Attach the zipper foot to the machine and stitch the zipper to the boxing strip, stitching about ⅜" (1 cm) from the teeth on both sides. Using a seam ripper, pick open the basted part of the seam to expose the zipper.

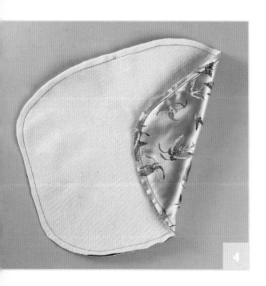

10 Pin a handle to each side of the bag on the right sides, aligning the ends to the marks.

11 Pin one long edge of the boxing strip to one curved edge of the bag, right sides together. Clip the seam allowance of the boxing strip as necessary to fit the curved edge of the bag; pin often. Stitch the strip to the bag, beginning and ending with backstitches exactly at the bottom stitching line of the bag.

12 Unzip the zipper. Repeat step 11 for the opposite side.

13 Clip the seam allowance of the bag at the bottom stitching lines up to the end of the stitching from steps 11 and 12 . Stitch the ends of the boxing strip to the bag bottom, beginning and ending at the ends of the other stitching lines. Trim and clean-finish the seam allowances. Turn the bag right side out.

8 Center an interfacing piece on the wrong side of two of the handle pieces. Fuse them in place. Pin the plain handles to the interfaced handles, right sides together. Stitch ½" (1.3 cm) seams on the long sides. Using a bodkin or tube turner, turn the handles right side out. Topstitch each long edge.

9 Pin the outer body/batting piece to the lining/pocket piece, wrong sides together. Baste through all layers ¼" (6 mm) from the edge. Through all layers, stitch on the bottom stitching lines (marked on the lining), crossing the pocket stitching lines.

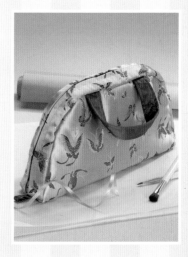

DESIGNER'S TIP

When sewing on vinyl, use a Teflon presser foot or place strips of tissue paper between the vinyl and presser foot to help the fabric feed smoothly.

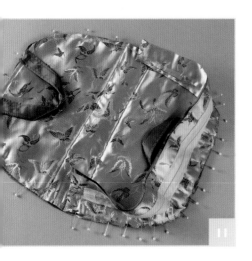

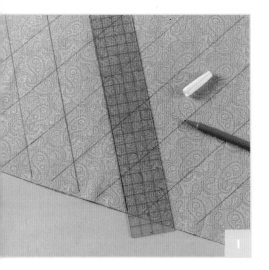

1 Cut a 21" (53.5 cm) square of each of the two fabrics. Using a fabric marking pen or pencil, mark a diagonal line (30 to 45 degrees) on the right side of one fabric square. Parallel to the first line, mark lines evenly spaced 1" to 2" (2.5 to 5 cm) apart across the entire piece. Repeat in the opposite direction.

2 Cut a 21" (53.5 cm) square of batting. Layer the batting between the fabric pieces, with the right sides of the fabric facing out. Pin the layers together around the edge and several places toward the center. Stitch through all layers along all the lines, working first in one direction and then the other, to make quilted fabric.

3 To make the pattern, draw an 18" × 19" (46 × 48.5 cm) rectangle on paper. Using a small plate as a guide, round off the corners of the pattern. Mark a fold line 5" (12.7 cm) from one short end. Cut out the pattern. Use the pattern to cut a piece from the quilted fabric.

4 Unfold the bias tape. Pin one edge of the tape to the edge of the quilted fabric, on either side. Stitch the tape to the fabric along the crease of the outer fold. Begin about 2" (5 cm) from the end of the tape and stop before you reach the beginning end again.

5 To join ends of tape, cut one end diagonally following the fabric grain. Mark a dotted line on the opposite end of the tape even with the diagonally cut edge. Mark a solid line ½" (1.3 cm) from the dotted line and cut the tape on the solid line.

6 Place the diagonally cut ends of the tape right sides together so the folds will align when you stitch the seam. Stitch ¼" (6 mm) seam. Press the seam allowances open. Finish sewing the tape to the quilted fabric.

7 Refold the bias tape, wrap it over the edge of the quilted fabric to the other side, and pin in place. Hand-stitch the free side of the bias tape in place.

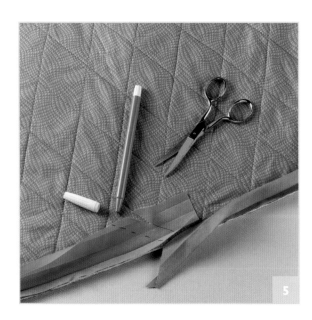

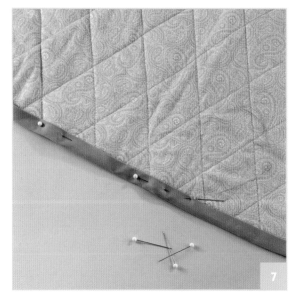

8 Turn up 5" (12.7 cm) on one long edge and pin. Flip the roll over, with the fold at the bottom. Turn back the right side 1½" (3.8 cm), and pin. Stitch through all layers along the inner edge of the bias tape to secure the narrow fold in place.

9 Slip both ends of the ribbon through both D-rings. Turn under the raw edges of the ribbon at the base of the D-rings and stitch the strap to roll at the center of the narrow flap.

10 With the bottom flap facing up, mark parallel stitching lines the desired distance apart on the flap. Stitch through all layers to form the pockets.

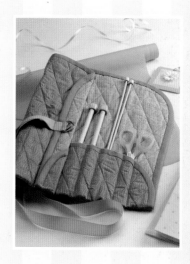

DESIGNER'S TIP

Speed up the assembly by starting with pre-quilted, reversible fabric.

BEACH BABE TOTE

MATERIALS

Copy machine or graph paper for enlarging pattern

Paper and pencil for drawing pattern

Carpenter's square or T-square ruler

Pencil-and-string compass

½ yd. (0.5 m) print canvas

¼ yd. (0.25 m) first coordinating solid color of canvas

2 yd. (1.85 m) second coordinating solid color of canvas

Contrasting thread

1 ¼ yd. (1.15 m) filler cord, 3/16" (4.5 mm) diameter

Welting foot or zipper foot

Hand-sewing needle

Eight silver grommets, 3/8" (1 cm) diameter, and application tool

Medium-weight fusible interfacing

2 yd. (1.85 m) cotton twisted cord, 3/8" (1 cm) diameter

Make a sunny gift for someone who loves going to the beach or hanging by the pool. This drawstring bag is large enough to hold everything for the day. The wide, sturdy handle makes carrying comfortable, and the grommeted tie holds it all inside. Tuck in a towel, hat, or sunscreen to enhance the gift.

FINISHED SIZE: 11" WIDE × 18" TALL (28 × 46 CM)

1 Enlarge the handle pattern on page 83, and cut it out. Draw these patterns using paper, pencil, a carpenter's square or T-square ruler, and a string-and-pencil compass:

> *Bag body:* rectangle 35½" wide × 14" tall (90.3 × 35.5 cm)
>
> *Top border:* rectangle 35½" wide × 3" tall (90.3 × 7.5 cm)
>
> *Bottom border:* rectangle 35½" wide × 4" tall (90.3 × 10 cm)
>
> *Base:* circle with 12" (30.5 cm) diameter
>
> *Lining:* rectangle 35½" wide × 17" tall (90.3 × 43 cm)

These patterns and dimensions include ½" (1.3 cm) seam allowances.

2 Cut one bag body from the print fabric. Cut two top borders from the first solid-color fabric. Cut one bottom border, two bases, one lining, and two handles from the second solid-color fabric. Also cut two 1⅞" × 20" (4.7 × 51 cm) bias strips for welting from the second solid-color fabric.

3 Pin the bottom border to the bottom of the bag body, right sides together. Stitch. Pin and stitch one top border to the top of the bag body. Press the seam allowances apart. Topstitch on both sides of each seam using contrasting thread. Pin the sides of the bag body, right sides together, matching border seams. Stitch, creating a cylinder. Set aside.

4 Stitch the bias welting strips together end-to-end and press the seam open. Encase the cotton filler cord inside the bias strip with wrong sides together and long raw edges of fabric even. Attach the zipper foot or welting foot to your sewing machine, and machine-baste close to the cord.

5 Pin the welting to the right side edge of one base piece, aligning the raw edges. Stitch, beginning a few inches from one end and stopping before you reach the beginning end again. The ends will overlap.

6 Cut one end of the welting straight across. Cut the other end so that it overlaps the first by about 2" (5 cm). Remove 2½" (6.5 cm) of the basting in the long end, exposing the filler cord. Trim the exposed cord so that it butts up against the trimmed and covered end of the cord. Wrap the fabric over both cord ends, turning under the raw edge to finish. Pin in place and finish basting the welting to the base. Set the welted base aside.

7 Pin the remaining top border to the upper edge of the lining, right sides together. Stitch. Press the seam open. Pin the sides of the lining, right sides together, matching border seams. Stitch, leaving a 12" (30.5 cm) opening in the center of the seam.

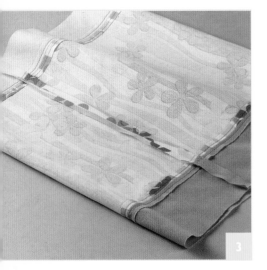

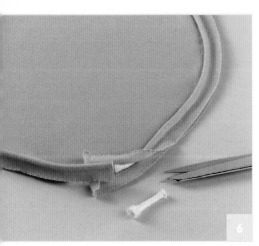

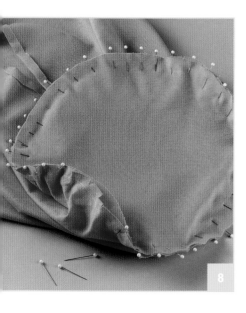

8 Stitch a line a scant ½" (1.3 cm) from the lower edge of the lining. Clip to the stitching line at ¾" (2 cm) intervals. Using plenty of pins, pin the lower edge of the lining to the remaining base piece, right sides together. The lining edge will spread at the clips to conform to the curved edge of the base. Stitch ½" (1.3 cm) seam. Set aside.

9 Repeat step 8 to attach the outer bag to the welted base.

10 With the outer bag right side out and the lining inside out, slip the outer bag into the lining and pin them together at the upper edge. Stitch, leaving a 2" (5 cm) opening centered over the back seam for inserting the handle later.

11 Turn the bag right side out through the large opening in the lining seam. Slipstitch the opening closed.

12 Pin the handle pieces right sides together and stitch the long, shaped seams. Trim the seam allowances, turn the handle right side out, and press. Insert the handle ends between the outer bag and lining through the opening in the upper edge at the back seam. The handle ends should extend slightly below the top border. Topstitch the upper edge, catching the handle in the stitching and closing the opening. Stitch over the topstitching on both sides of the border seam, stitching through the handle ends to secure.

13 Following the manufacturer's instructions, attach a grommet in the center of the top border, 2¼" (6 cm) on each side of the back seam. Attach six more grommets evenly spaced around the border.

14 Lace the decorative cotton cord through the grommets as in the photo on page 17.

DESIGNER'S TIP

When using large grommets, interface the fabric for extra support. Practice applying a few grommets on scrap fabric before working on your project.

TWO-STORY TOTE

MATERIALS

Paper and pencil for drawing pattern

Carpenter's square or T-square ruler

½ yd. (0.5 m) polka-dot fabric

½ yd. (0.5 m) lining fabric

¾ yd. (0.7 m) striped fabric

1½ yd. (1.4 m) medium-weight fusible interfacing, optional

Thread

Two separating, nylon sport zippers, 12" (30.5 cm) long

Seam ripper

Hand-sewing needle

1½ yd. (1.4 m) webbing, 1" (2.5 cm) wide

Four buttons, 1" (2.5 cm) diameter

Stiff cardboard or foam core board

This tote has a "downstairs" to keep a pair of shoes separate from everything else. Everyone needs a fun tote—and this one is a particularly good gift for a woman who commutes or is always on the go.

FINISHED SIZE: 11" WIDE × 14" TALL × 6½" DEEP (28 × 35.5 × 16.3 CM)

1 Draw these patterns using paper, pencil, and a carpenter's square or T-square ruler:

> *Top front:* rectangle 25" wide × 11" tall (63.5 × 28 cm)
>
> *Top back:* rectangle 12" wide × 11" tall (30.5 × 28 cm)
>
> *Bottom front:* rectangle 25" wide × 5" tall (63.5 × 12.7 cm)
>
> *Bottom back:* rectangle 12" wide × 5" tall (30.5 × 12.7 cm)
>
> *Base:* rectangle 12" wide × 7½" deep (30.5 × 19.3 cm)

Dimensions include ½" (1.3 cm) seam allowances.

2 Cut one top front, one top back, and one base from polka-dot fabric. Cut one top front, one top back, and one base from lining fabric. Cut two bottom fronts, two bottom backs, and two bases from striped fabric. To reinforce lightweight fabrics and strengthen the bases, cut one each of the top front, top back, bottom front, and bottom back and two bases from interfacing. Fuse the interfacing to the wrong sides of all the pieces.

3 Pin one long edge of the top front to the bottom front, right sides together. Machine-baste, using ½" (1.3 cm) seam allowances. Press the seam open.

4 Pin the two zippers, right side up, on the right side of the assembled piece, with the zipper teeth centered over the seam and the pull tabs centered in front. Overlap the tops of the zipper tapes so the ends of the tapes are ½" (1.3 cm) from sides of the fabric. Stitch the zippers in place close to the outer edges, taking care not to catch the seam allowances underneath.

5 Unzip the zippers. Using a seam ripper, pick open the basted seam to separate the top from the bottom. Set the bottom aside. Fold up the zipper tape on the front, and pin it away from the seam allowance.

6 Pin the top front to the top back, right sides together, along the short sides. Stitch, stopping and backstitching ½" (1.3 cm) from the lower edge on each seam. Press the seams open.

7 Pin the top to the polka-dot base, right sides together, aligning the center fronts and center backs. The seams of the top section should align to the back corners of the base. Clip into the seam allowance of the top to allow it to spread at the front corners of the base. Stitch the front and side edges only, leaving the back edge open.

8 Repeat steps 6 and 7 for the lining of the top front, back, and base.

9 Pin the upper edge of the assembled top to the upper edge of the assembled lining, right sides together, matching seams. Stitch the upper edge.

10 Turn the top right side out through one of the back openings. Press. Topstitch the upper edge. Set the top aside.

11 Pin the bottom front to the bottom back, right sides together, along the short sides. Stitch, starting and stopping by backstitching ½" (1.3 cm) from the upper and lower edges on each seam. Press the seams open.

12 Place the two striped bases, wrong sides together, and pin-baste the edges. Pin the assembled bottom to the pin-basted base, right sides together, aligning the center fronts and center backs. The seams of the bottom section should align to the back corners of the base. Clip into the seam allowance of the bottom to allow it to spread at the front corners of the base. Stitch the front and side edges only, leaving the back edge open.

13 Assemble the remaining striped bottom front and back pieces, as in step 11, for the bottom lining. Pin the lining to the base on the opposite side of the assembled bottom, clipping the seam allowances at the front corners. Stitch.

14 Turn the bottom right side out. Pin the back edges of the top (including the lining and base) to the back edge of the bottom (not including the lining), right sides together. Stitch. Turn under the upper seam allowances of the bottom lining, and slipstitch in place to cover the raw edges.

15 Zip the top and bottom together. Cut the webbing in half to make two handles. Turn under the ends and stitch one handle to the center front and one to the center back, with the ends about 6" (15 cm) apart. Stitch a button at each end of the handles.

16 To help support the base of the tote and the base of the shoe section, cut two 6½" × 11" (16.3 × 28 cm) rectangles from stiff cardboard or foam core board and place into position on each floor.

DESIGNER'S TIP

Since zipper colors are limited, choose your zipper color first and then have fun selecting three colorful, coordinating fabrics.

LUXURY SHOE BAGS

MATERIALS

(For one pair)

Paper and pencil for drawing pattern

Carpenter's square or T-square ruler

⅝ yd. (0.6 m) faux suede, 60" (152.5 cm) wide

Fabric marking pen or pencil

3" (7.5 cm) Velcro, ¾" (2 cm) wide

Thread

Fusible letter appliqués, 1" (2.5 cm) tall

When the frequent travelers in your life are on the road, remind them that you're thinking of them with these luxurious shoe bags. The generously sized shoe bags will also be a hit with someone who cultivates a well-organized closet. The bags are made of light, washable faux suede and feature Velcro closures and press-on monograms.

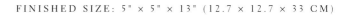

FINISHED SIZE: 5" × 5" × 13" (12.7 × 12.7 × 33 CM)

1 Draw two patterns using paper, pencil, and a carpenter's square or T-square ruler:

Bag body: rectangle 21" tall × 17" wide (53.5 × 43 cm). Draw vertical fold lines on the pattern 3" (7.5 cm) from the long cut edges. Draw two more fold lines dividing the center into three 5" (12.7 cm) spaces.

Flap: rectangle 10" tall × 6" wide (25.5 × 15 cm). Angle the corners by drawing diagonal lines 2" (5 cm) up and over from each corner.

These dimensions include 1/2" (1.3 cm) seam allowances.

2 Cut one bag body and two flaps for each shoe bag. Transfer fold lines to the right side of the bag body, using a fabric marking pen or pencil. Mark placement for Velcro in the center of the body, 3 1/2" (9 cm) from the top and in the center of the flap, 1 1/4" (3.2 cm) from the bottom.

3 Cut a 1 1/2" (3.8 cm) piece of Velcro. Stitch the hook side to the right side of the bag body at the mark. Stitch the loop side to the right side of one flap section at the mark.

4 Fold the bag body in half lengthwise, right sides together. Stitch the back seam; pivot at the corner and stitch the bottom seam. Trim the seam allowances to 1/4" (6 mm).

5 To create a paper-bag bottom for the shoe bag, fold the lower corner, aligning the bottom seam over the back seam. Measure along the bottom seam 2 1/2" (6.5 cm) from the point, and draw a line perpendicular to the seams. The line should be 5" (12.7 cm) long. Stitch on the marked line through all layers, keeping the seam allowances on both sides turned open. Trim away the triangle 1/4" (6 mm) from the stitching line. Repeat for the other corner, centering the bottom seam in the 5" (12.7 cm) stitching line.

6 Pin two flap pieces right sides together. Stitch the sides and angled bottom, leaving the other end open. Trim the seam allowances.

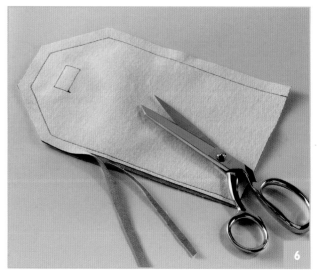

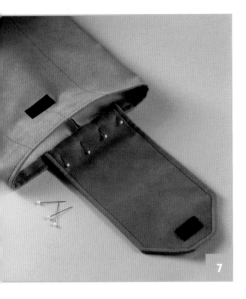

DESIGNER'S TIP

The bag is sized for a
man's shoe up to size 12.
Simply shorten or lengthen
the body to fit smaller or
larger shoes.

7 Turn the bag body and flap right side out. Turn under ½" (1.3 cm) on the upper edge of the bag body. Topstitch ¼" (6 mm) from the fold. Topstitch ¼" (6 mm) from the outer seamed edges of the flap. Center the open end of the flap over the back seam of the body, aligning the raw edges. Topstitch the flap to the body over the previous stitching line.

8 Fold the body along the marked lines, and pin. Topstitch ¼" (6 mm) from the folds, stopping and back-stitching ¼" (6 mm) from the bottom corners. Fold, pin, and stitch a crease in each edge at the base of the bag, starting and stopping with backstitches at the ends of the previous stitching lines.

9 Fuse the monogram letters to the flaps.

FIRST-PLACE
STADIUM CUSHION

MATERIALS

Paper and pencil for drawing pattern

Carpenter's square or T-square ruler

Pencil-and-string compass

½ yd. (0.5 m) light color fabric

1¼ yd. (1.15 m) dark color fabric

Matching and contrasting thread

15" (38 cm) square of fabric in each of two ball colors:

(black and white = soccer)

(red and white = baseball)

(brown and white = football)

(brown and black = basketball)

½ yd. (0.5 m) paper-backed fusible web

Fabric marking pen or pencil

4 yd. (3.7 m) filler cord, ⅜" (1 cm) diameter

Welting foot, optional

8" (20.5 cm) webbing, 1" (2.5 cm) wide

Hand-sewing needle

15" × 17" × 3" (38 × 43 × 7.5 cm) foam

1 yd. (0.92 m) lightweight upholstery batting, optional

No more hard, cold bleacher seats for some lucky sports fan! Easy to carry and full of team spirit, this stadium cushion will provide hours of comfort at sporting events. Make the cushion in the fan's team colors and add a soccer, baseball, basketball, or football theme using one of the appliqué patterns provided on pages 84 and 85. Parents who go to lots of youth games would love one, too!

FINISHED SIZE: 15" × 17" × 3" (38 × 43 × 7.5 CM)

1 Trace the soccer ball appliqué pattern(s) on page 84 or enlarge desired patterns on page 85, and cut them out. Draw these patterns using paper, pencil, a carpenter's square or T-square ruler, and a string-and-pencil compass:

Front: rectangle 9½" wide × 8½" tall (24.3 × 21.8 cm)

Back: rectangle 18" wide × 16" tall (46 × 40.5 cm)

Boxing strip: rectangle 4" wide × 33" long (10 × 84 cm)

Ball: circle with 10" (25.5 cm) diameter

Dimensions include ½" (1.3 cm) seam allowances.

2 Cut two front pieces and two boxing strips from light fabric. Cut two fronts and one back from dark fabric. Also cut four 1⅞" × 35" (4.7 × 89 cm) bias strips for welting from the dark fabric.

3 Stitch a light front to a dark front, right sides together, along the shorter sides. Repeat for the second set. Press the seams open. Stitch the two sets right sides together, matching the seams and alternating color placement.

4 Fuse paper-backed web to the wrong side of the ball fabrics, following the manufacturer's instructions. Trace the appliqué patterns on the paper backing of the appropriate fabrics. Cut out the shapes. Peel away the paper backing from the shapes. Fuse the ball to the center of the assembled front. Fuse other appliqué pieces in place. For the soccer ball, fuse the pentagons in place, spacing the edge pieces evenly. Use a fabric marker to draw lines connecting the points of the pentagons, as in the photo on page 29.

5 Set the sewing machine for a zigzag or appliqué stitch with a medium width and very short length. Using contrasting thread, satin stitch all the raw edges and design lines.

6 Stitch two bias welting strips together end-to-end and press the seam open. Encase the cotton filler cord inside the bias strip with wrong sides together and long raw edges of fabric even. Attach the zipper foot or welting foot to your sewing machine, and machine-baste close to the cord.

7 Pin the welting to the right side edge of the cushion front, beginning in the center on one side and aligning the raw edges. Clip into the welting seam allowance at the corners to allow it to spread and turn the corner smoothly. Stitch, beginning a few inches from one end and stopping before you reach the beginning end again. The ends will overlap.

8 Cut one end of the welting straight across. Cut the other end so that it overlaps the first by about 2" (5 cm). Remove 2½" (6.5 cm) of the basting in the long end exposing the filler cord. Trim the exposed cord so that it butts up against the trimmed and covered end of the cord. Wrap the fabric over both cord ends, turning under the raw edge to finish. Pin in place and finish basting the welting to the front. (see the photo on page 18, step 6).

9 Repeat steps 6 to 8 for the cushion back.

10 Locate the center of one boxing strip, and mark points 2½" (6.5 cm) to each side of center for the handle placement. Turn under ½" (1.3 cm) on each end of the webbing handle and stitch securely to the boxing strip at the marks.

11 Stitch the boxing strips together end-to-end to make a ring. Press the seams open. Pin the boxing strip to the cushion front, centering the seams at the sides and the handle at the top, and sandwiching the welting between the fabrics. Clip into the boxing strip seam allowance at the corners to allow it to spread and turn the corner smoothly. Stitch.

12 Repeat step 11 to attach the other side of the boxing strip to the cushion back. Leave an opening in one side at least 15" (38 cm) long.

13 Turn the cushion cover right side out through the opening.

14 For a softer cushion, wrap the foam in batting, cutting the edges to just meet. Hand-stitch the edges together.

15 Insert the foam into the cushion cover and slipstitch the opening closed.

DESIGNER'S TIP

To speed up the project, buy fabric-covered decorator's welting in a color that coordinates with your fabrics.

CUSTOM NECKTIE

MATERIALS

Copy machine or graph paper for enlarging pattern

Paper and pencil for drawing pattern

7/8 yd. (0.8 m) lightweight silk or synthetic fabric

1/4 yd. (0.25 m) lining fabric

7/8 yd. (0.8 m) non-fusible woven interfacing or wool underlining

Thread

Fabric marking pen or pencil

Hand-sewing needle

2 1/2" (6.5 cm) satin ribbon, 3/4" (2 cm) wide

Next Father's Day, don't buy him a tie—make him one. Choose silk in a traditional pattern or a novelty print about something he loves, like fishing, golf, or wine. For a finishing touch, embroider his name or initials on the ribbon that holds the tail.

FINISHED SIZE: 3 1/2" AT THE WIDEST END × 58" LONG (9 × 147 CM)

1 Enlarge the four tie patterns on pages 86 and 87, and cut them out. Draw a long line on paper and place the center line of the two tie front patterns on the line, with the inner edges of the patterns 20" (51 cm) apart. Connect the lines to complete the pattern. Repeat for the tie back patterns, spacing them 16" (40.5 cm) apart. Trace the interfacing patterns from the centers of the tie patterns. Enlarge the lining patterns on page 88. All patterns include 1/4" (6 mm) seam allowances.

2 Placing all patterns on the bias, cut one tie front and one tie back from the outer fabric, one front lining and one back lining from the lining fabric, and one front interfacing and one back interfacing.

3 Stitch the narrow ends of the front and back outer tie, right sides together. Trim the seam allowances and press them open.

4 Transfer the two pairs of dots to the wrong side of fabric at the front and back points, using a fabric marking pen or pencil. Fold the pointed end of the tie front in half lengthwise, right sides together, matching the dots. Stitch the short distance from the dots to the fold, backstitching at both ends. Repeat for the tie back.

5 Open the fold and pin the front lining to the front tie, right sides together, matching the angled edges. Stitch the two angled edges, breaking the stitches at the point and beginning again on the other side of the small stitched pleat. Trim the seam. Repeat for the pointed end of the tie back.

6 Roll the seams of the front point inward 1/4" (6 mm) and pin them in place. Do not press. Stitch the sides of the lining piece to the sides of the tie with 1/4" (6 mm) seams. Repeat for the other point.

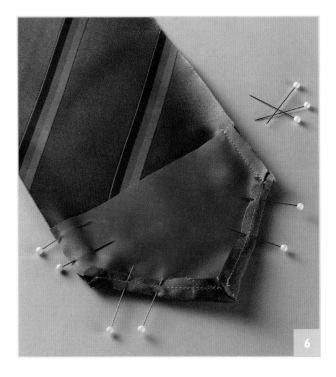

7 Turn the points to the right side and press very lightly, pushing the seam allowances toward the lining.

8 Stitch the interfacing together by overlapping the ends and zigzagging. Slip the interfacing under the linings and pin it to the tie, centering it along the entire length.

9 Fold one long edge of the tie over the interfacing and hand-stitch the edge to the interfacing. Turn the other edge under ½" (1.3 cm) and pin. Fold the pinned edge over the interfacing and hand-stitch the fold to the center of the tie, catching the interfacing underneath but not the tie front.

10 Turn under the ends of the ribbon, and hand-stitch them to the back of the tie front 8" (20.5 cm) from the point.

DESIGNER'S TIP

Choose a lightweight luxury fabric like silk. Select a solid color or a small print, keeping in mind the fabric will be cut diagonally.

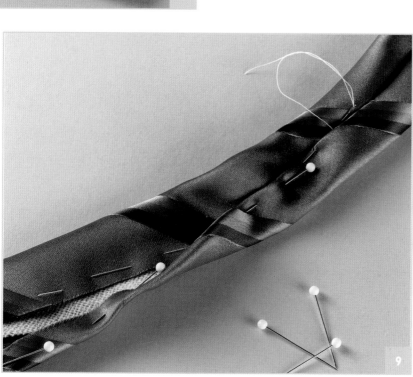

FRIENDLY ELEPHANT BIB

MATERIALS

Copy machine or graph paper for enlarging pattern

Paper and pencil for drawing pattern

½ yd. (0.5 m) lightweight terry cloth

⅜ yd. (0.35 m) solid or subtle print fabric, 44" (112 cm) wide

Pink felt, 2" (5 cm) square

Lightweight quilt batting, 8" × 12" (20.5 × 30.5 cm)

Thread

6" (15 cm) grosgrain ribbon, ⅞" (2.2 cm) wide

Hand-sewing needle

⅝" (1.5 cm) Velcro, 1" (2.5 cm) wide

Black embroidery floss and needle

2½ yd. (2.3. m) double-fold bias tape

Pacifier with loop handle

Here's a unique and thoughtful baby gift. While the bib protects clothing, the elephant keeps track of a pacifier— no more searching everywhere for it. Choose a fabric in pink, blue, or unisex pastels like green or yellow.

FINISHED SIZE: 11" × 12" (28 × 30.5 CM)

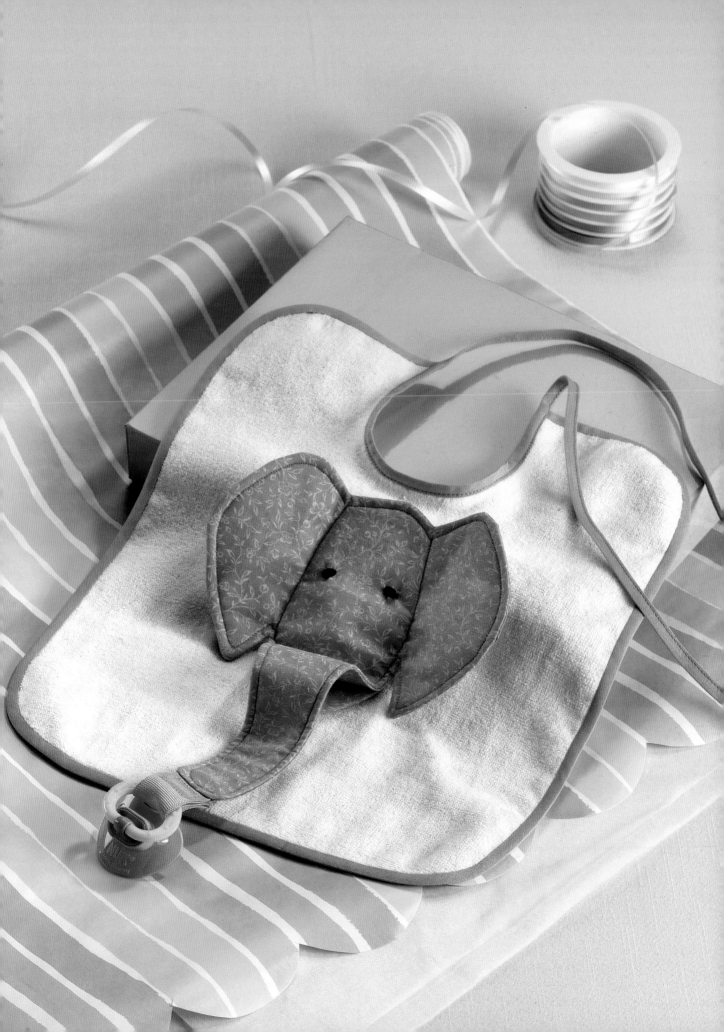

1 Enlarge the bib, elephant, mouth, and tongue patterns found on pages 89, 90, and 91, and cut them out. Patterns include ¼" (6 mm) seam allowances.

2 Cut one bib from terry cloth. Cut two elephants and two mouths from fabric. Cut one tongue from pink felt. Cut one elephant from batting.

3 Pin or baste quilt batting to the wrong side of one elephant piece along the edges.

4 Fold ribbon in half crosswise. Aligning cut edges, pin the ribbon to the right side of the end of the elephant's trunk.

5 Pin the elephants right sides together, sandwiching the ribbon between them. Stitch ¼" (6 mm) from all edges, leaving a 3" (7.5 cm) opening along the

straight section of an ear. Clip up to the seam at corners.

6 Pin the two mouth pieces right sides together. Stitch the long curved edge.

7 Turn the elephant and mouth pieces right side out. Slipstitch the openings closed and press flat.

8 Topstitch the elephant ¼" (6 mm) from the outer edge. Stitch one side of the Velcro to the underside of the ribbon, through both layers, just below the trunk. Stitch the other side to the underside of the ribbon just above the fold. Embroider the eyes.

9 Unfold the bias tape and pin the edge with the narrower fold to the right side of the bib edge, beginning and ending at the neck edges. Stitch in the crease of the fold.

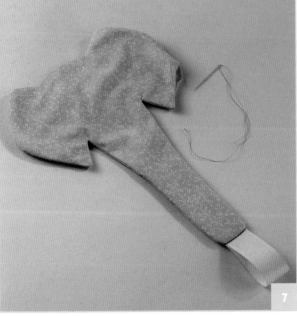

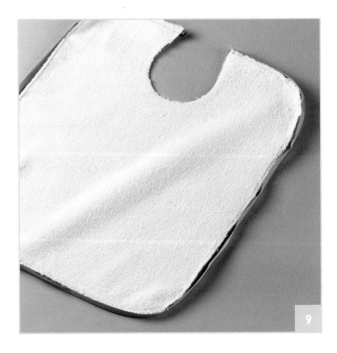

10 Wrap the bias tape to the back of the bib, encasing the raw edge. Pin the tape, with the fold just covering the stitching line. Slipstitch the fold in place.

11 Cut a 1-yd. (0.92 m) length of bias tape. Repeat steps 9 and 10 at the neck edge, centering the tape to the neck to finish the raw edge and create bib ties. Beginning at the end of one tie, topstitch close to the folds of the tape, continuing the stitching around the neck edge to the end of the other tie.

12 Stitch the mouth to the center of the bib, 4" (10 cm) below the neck edge. Pin the tongue to the upper straight edge of the mouth, and stitch in place.

13 Pin the elephant head on the bib, over the mouth, and stitch through all layers between the head and ears. Wrap the ribbon around the pacifier, and press the Velcro pieces together to secure.

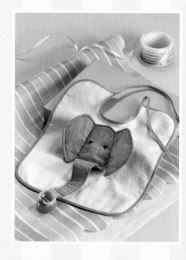

DESIGNER'S TIP

You can speed up the project by buying a bib and choosing elephant fabric to match. Coordinate the pacifier, too!

CURLY SOFT BEAR

A teddy bear is a gift of love and comfort for anyone, from newborn to ninety. Faux fur is available in a wide variety of fun colors and textures and is a forgiving fabric for a beginning sewer. Making and giving this teddy will be as much fun as receiving one.

This teddy has button eyes. Use safety eyes if your gift is for a baby or small child.

FINISHED SIZE: 17" (43 CM) TALL

1 Enlarge the nine bear patterns on pages 91 and 92, and cut them out. Trace the arm pattern a second time and cut it off where indicated for the underarm. Patterns include 1/4" (6 mm) seam allowances.

2 Cut two ears, two paws, and two soles from soft fur. Cut four legs, one nose, and two each of the remaining pieces (including two ears) from curly fur. Be sure to cut mirror-image pieces of those that are multiples. (Either cut the pieces with the fabric folded right sides together or flip the pattern over when cutting a single layer of fabric.) Transfer all marks.

3 Pin a paw to the straight lower edge of the underarm, right sides together; stitch. Stitch the upper arm to the lower arm, leaving a 4" (10 cm) opening on the long edge. Repeat for the other arm. Turn the arms right side out.

4 Stitch the front pieces together along the center front. Stitch the darts in the back pieces; turn them upward. Stitch the back pieces together along the center back. Pin the front to the back on the sides and stitch.

5 Pin two leg pieces together on the curved edge, and stitch. Pin the straight edges together and stitch, leaving a 4" (10 cm) opening in the center of the seam. Pin the sole to the lower edge of the leg, and stitch. Repeat for the other leg. Turn the legs right side out.

6 Match up the front and back seams of one leg and pin flat. Pin the leg to the lower edge of the assembled body, sandwiched between the front and back. Make sure the toes are pointing forward. Pin the other leg into position. Stitch across the bottom of the body through all layers. Turn the body right side out.

7 Pin a curly fur ear to a soft fur ear along the curved edge, and stitch. Repeat for second ear. Turn the ears right side out.

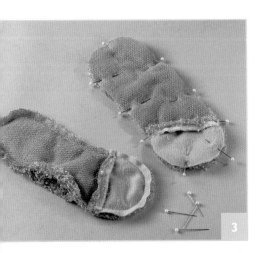

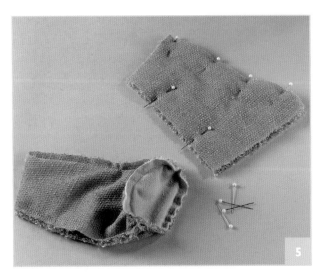

10 Stitch button eyes to the face. If the bear is for a small child, attach safety eyes instead. Cut a small triangle of felt for the nose tip. Stitch it to the point of the nose, using embroidery thread.

11 Using two buttons as washers, stitch the underarm to the shoulder of the body at the side seam. Work through the neck opening to get inside the body and through the opening in the back seam of the arm. Stitch back and forth through the button holes several times to attach the arm securely. Repeat for the other arm.

12 Stuff the legs and arms with fiberfill and slipstitch the openings closed.

13 Machine-stitch the front of the body to the front of the head at the neck edge, stitching just beyond the side seams. Stuff the body and head. Slipstitch the back neck opening closed.

14 Wrap the ribbon around the bear's neck and tie a big bow in the front.

8 Stitch the head side pieces together at the center front. Pin the top of the center front seam to the point of the nose, and finish pinning the nose edges to the upper edges of the head sides. Stitch. Stitch the head back pieces together at the center back.

9 Pin the ears to the upper edge of the head front assembly, leaving 1 ½" (3.8 cm) between them and making sure the soft fur faces forward. Stitch the head back to the head front assembly, catching the ears in the seam.

PUPPY-DOG
HAT AND SCARF

MATERIALS

Copy machine or graph paper for enlarging pattern

Paper and pencil for drawing pattern

Carpenter's square or T-square ruler

⅝ yd. (0.6 m) colored fleece

Thread

Two stuffed or bean animals, about 6" (15 cm) long

Hand-sewing needle

3 yd. (2.75 m) narrow ribbon or trim

¼ yd. (0.25 m) white fleece

Make a child giggle with this fun set. All you need is fleece and a pair of little stuffed animals.

I Enlarge the hat crown pattern on page 93, and cut it out. Draw two patterns using paper, pencil, and a carpenter's square or T-square ruler:

> *Scarf:* rectangle 6" × 50"
> (15 × 127 cm)
>
> *Hat brim:* rectangle 6" × 23"
> (15 × 58.5 cm)

Dimensions include ½" (1.3 cm) seam allowances.

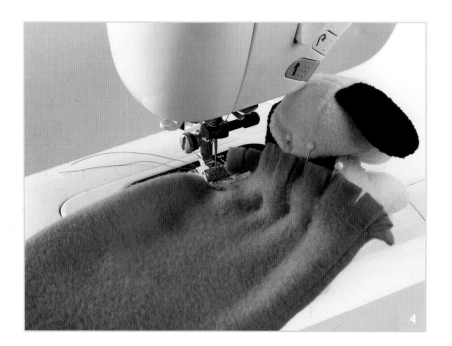

SCARF

I Cut two scarf pieces from the colored fleece.

2 Pin the two scarf pieces right sides together, along the long edges. Stitch, starting and stopping ¾" (2 cm) from the short ends. Knot the thread tails securely at the ends of the seams.

3 Fringe the short ends of the scarf by making cuts ¾" (2 cm) deep and ½" (1.3 cm) apart. Turn the scarf right side out.

4 Coax the stuffing away from the center of the animal and cut the animal in half. Baste each side closed. Pin one end of the animal between the fringed layers at one end of the scarf, just beyond the fringe. Stitch through all layers by hand or machine. Repeat at the other end.

5 Cut ribbon into four lengths, each 27" (68.5 cm) long. Tie one length of ribbon into a bow around each end of the scarf over the stitching.

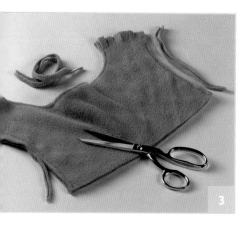

crown. Knot the thread tails securely at the ends of the seams.

3 Fringe the short ends of the crown by making cuts ¾" (2 cm) deep and ½" (1.3 cm) apart. Trim seams and turn the crown right side out.

4 Pin the short ends of the brim together and stitch, forming a circle. Pin one edge of the brim to the lower edge of the crown, right sides together. Stitch.

5 Turn the hat inside out. Fold the brim in half lengthwise. Turn under ½" (1.3 cm) on the cut edge of the brim and pin it over the seam line. Slipstitch the fold in place.

6 Attach animal halves to the short ends of the crown, as in step 4 for the scarf. Tie the two remaining lengths of ribbon over the stitches.

HAT

1 Cut two crowns from the colored fleece. Cut one brim from the white fleece.

2 Pin the crown pieces, right sides together, on the curved sides and top seams. Stitch, starting and stopping ¾" (2 cm) from the short ends of the

DESIGNER'S TIP

The brim of this hat is 22" (56 cm) around. For a perfect fit, measure the circumference of the child's head and alter the length of the brim and width of the crown by pinching or splitting each pattern in the center.

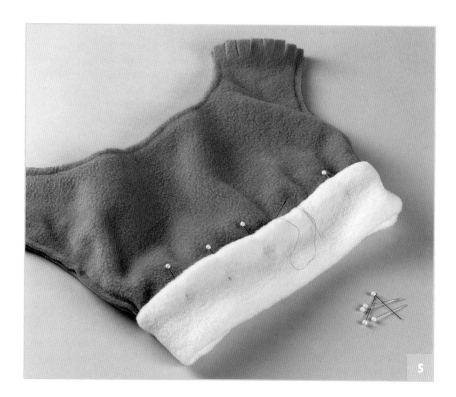

CHARMED SOCKS

Charm a little girl by decorating socks with dangling beads and personalized charms. You start with plain socks—choose ones with stretchy rib knit cuffs. The "lettuce edging" is done with a simple zigzag stitch while you stretch the socks as much as possible.

MATERIALS

(For one pair)

Pair of colored socks

Fabric marking pen or pencil

Ruler

Contrasting thread

28-gauge craft wire

Wire cutter

20 charms, 1/2" (1.3 cm)

30 colored glass beads, 6 to 8 mm

50 metal beads, 6 to 8 mm

20 metal double rings, 7 mm

Hand-sewing needle, optional

1 Mark three lines on the ribbed cuff about 1 1/2" (3.8 cm) apart, beginning at least 3/4" (2 cm) from the top, using a fabric marking pen or pencil. Turn the sock inside out.

2 Set the sewing machine for a zigzag stitch with medium width and short length. Fold the cuff down along the top marked line. Place the fold under the presser foot and, with one hand in front and one in back, stretch the folded edge. Zigzag along the fold, allowing the left swing of the needle to go into the sock and the right swing of the needle to go over the edge. Stop as necessary to reposition your hands. Repeat at each marked line.

3 To make the beaded dangles, cut 10 pieces of wire, each 12" (30.5 cm) long and 10 pieces of wire each 8" (20.5

cm) long. String a charm onto the center of each wire and twist the wire ends together. String three metal beads and two glass beads on each of the longer twisted wires, alternating metal and glass; string two metal beads and one glass bead on the shorter wires. Add a wire ring at the top of each dangle and twist the wire ends tightly to secure. Cut off the excess wire.

4 Stitch the dangles randomly to the lettuce-edged folds, either by hand or by machine.

BALLERINA TUTU

MATERIALS

3 yd. (2.75 m) sheer fabric

Yardstick (meterstick) or tape measure

Thread

4 yd. (3.7 m) heavy-duty thread or lightweight string

1 package extra-wide double-fold bias tape

3 yd. (2.75 m) feather boa trim

Hand-sewing needle

1 1/8 yd. (1.05 m) strung imitation pearls, 1/8" (3 mm) diameter

1 1/4 yd. (1.15 m) satin ribbon, 3/8" (9 mm) wide

1 1/4 yd. (1.15 m) sheer ribbon, 7/8" (23 mm) wide

15 assorted buttons, bows, and ribbon-rose novelties

Glue, optional

The first thing a little girl will do in this skirt is twirl and twirl! Select a sheer fabric with embroidery and ornamentation or choose inexpensive netting, then embellish with ribbons and pearls. She'll feel so special!

FINISHED SIZE: 24" WAIST, 10" LENGTH
(61 × 25.5 CM)

1 Straighten the cut ends of the sheer fabric, if necessary. Cut two rectangles 11" (28 cm) wide the full length of the sheer fabric.

2 Turn under 1" (2.5 cm) on one long edge of one piece, and press. Tuck in the cut edge to meet the crease and press again, creating a ½" (1.3 cm) double-fold hem. Stitch along the inner fold. Repeat for one long edge of the other piece. Then stitch double-fold hems in the short ends of both pieces.

3 Layer the two long pieces right side up, aligning the upper raw edges. Pin. Set the sewing machine for a wide, long zigzag stitch. Working from the right side, stitch the layers together along the entire long edge, ¼" (6 mm) from the cut edges, zigzagging over a heavy thread or thin cord. Pull the cord to gather the skirt edge to a length of 24" (61 cm). Secure each end of the gathering cord by wrapping the thread in figure-eight fashion around a pin.

4 Cut 2½ yd. (2.3 m) of the bias tape and mark off the center 24" (61 cm). Unfold the tape. Pin the wrong side of the gathered skirt edge to one edge of the tape between the marks, distributing the fullness evenly.

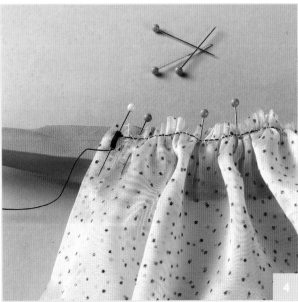

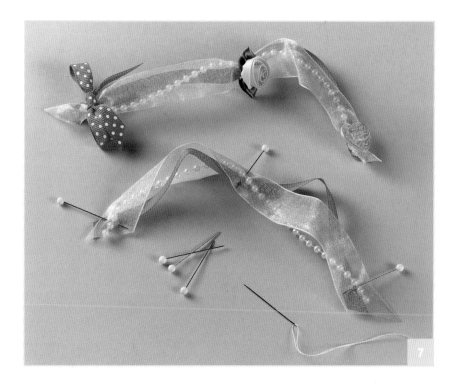

DESIGNER'S TIP

The anticipation of the completed project will become even greater if you allow the child to select her own buttons and ribbons for a surprise gift yet to come.

5 Stitch the tape to the skirt, stitching in the crease of the first fold. Wrap the tape to the wrong side, encasing the raw edges. Pin the tape, with the fold just covering the stitching line. Slipstitch the fold in place. Beginning at the end of one tie, topstitch close to the folds of the tape, continuing the stitching above the skirt to the end of the other tie.

6 Hand-stitch boa feathers to the hem of the top skirt, catching the boa at the beginning and end and every few inches.

7 Cut the pearls into five 8" (20.5 cm) lengths. Cut the ribbons into five 9" (23 cm) lengths. Group a sheer ribbon, a satin ribbon, and a pearl string, and hand-tack them together at both ends and at the center. Stitch or glue a novelty button or bow at each stitched location. Repeat to make four more ribbon embellishments.

8 Hand-tack the ribbon embellishments, evenly spaced, to the waistline of the skirt.

MY OWN LUNCH BAG

MATERIALS

Paper and pencil for drawing pattern

Carpenter's square or T-square ruler

¾ yd. (0.7 m) nylon sport fabric

¼ yd. (0.25 m) nylon sport fabric, in contrasting color

⅜ yd. (0.35 m) temperature insulated batting

¼ yd. (0.25 m) non-woven interfacing

3" (7.5 cm) Velcro, ¾" (2 cm) wide

Thread

Fabric marking pen or pencil

⅝ yd. (0.6 m) nylon webbing, 1" (2.5 cm) wide

Fusible or press-on monogram letters, 1½" (3.8 cm) high

A bright, insulated lunch bag is a perfect gift for a kid. When it's time for lunch, there will be no mistaking this personalized lunch bag from the others. It's roomy and wipes clean. An outside pocket holds milk money or a note from Mom or Dad.

FINISHED SIZE: 7½" WIDE × 10" TALL × 3½" DEEP (19.3 × 25.5 × 9 CM)

1 Draw two patterns using paper, pencil, and a carpenter's square or T-square ruler:

> *Bag body:* rectangle 2¾" tall × 12" wide (32.4 × 30.5 cm)
>
> *Pocket:* rectangle 9" tall × 6½" wide (23 × 16.3 cm)

Enlarge the pocket flap and lid on page 94, and cut them out. Dimensions include ½" (1.3 cm) seam allowances.

2 Using the patterns, cut four bag bodies and one pocket from the colored fabric. Cut two pocket flaps and two lids from the contrasting fabric. Cut two bodies and one lid from batting. Cut one pocket and one pocket flap from interfacing. Cut two lengths of Velcro, each 1½" (3.8 cm) long.

3 Machine-baste interfacing to the wrong side of one pocket flap, ¼" (6 mm) from the edges. Trim the interfacing close to the stitches. Center the loop tape on the right side of the other pocket flap, 1¾" (4.5 cm) below the upper edge. Stitch the tape to the flap along the edges.

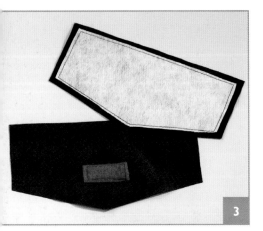

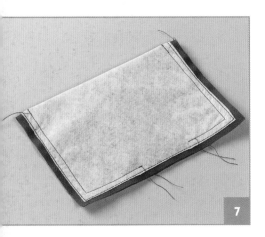

4 Pin the flaps right sides together. Stitch along the edges, leaving a 4" (10 cm) opening in the center of the upper edge. Trim the seam allowances and clip the corners diagonally. Turn the flap right side out and press. Topstitch the sides and angled lower edge.

5 Machine-baste the batting to the wrong side of one lid flap, ¼" (6 mm) from the edges. Trim the batting close to the stitches. Center the loop tape on the right side of the other lid flap, 5¼" (13.2 cm) below the long straight edge. Stitch the tape to the lid around all edges.

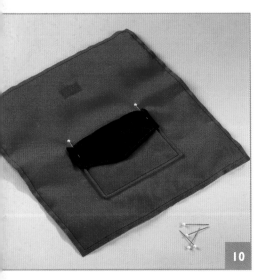

6 Pin the lids right sides together. Stitch along the edges, leaving a 4" (10 cm) opening in the center of the upper edge. Trim the seam allowances and clip the corners diagonally. Turn the lid right side out and press. Topstitch the sides and angled lower edge.

7 Machine-baste interfacing to the wrong side of one pocket, ¼" (6 mm) from all edges. Trim the interfacing close to the stitches. Fold the pocket in half crosswise, right sides together, and stitch all edges, leaving a small opening centered along one edge. Trim the seam allowances and clip the corners diagonally. Turn the pocket right side out and press.

8 Center the hook tape on the right side of the pocket, ¾" (2 cm) below the folded edge. Stitch the tape to the pocket along the edges.

9 Machine-baste the batting to the wrong side of each bag body, ¼" (6 mm) from the edges. Trim the batting close to the stitches.

10 Pin the pocket to the right side of one body, centering it with the open (lower) edge 2½" (6.5 cm) from the lower edge of the body. Topstitch the pocket in place on the sides and lower edge. Pin the pocket flap above the pocket and topstitch in place along the upper edge, taking care not to catch the pocket in the stitches. Center the hook tape 2" (5 cm) below the upper edge of the body and stitch in place.

DESIGNER'S TIP

Interline your lunch bag with a standard quilt batting or choose a batting that contains a hot/cold reflecting layer for added insulation.

11 Pin the two body pieces right sides together along the sides and lower edge. Stitch. Trim the corners diagonally and press the seams open.

12 To create a paper-bag bottom for the lunch bag, fold the lower corner, aligning the bottom seam over the side seam. Measure along the bottom seam 1¾" (4.5 cm) from the point, and draw a line perpendicular to the seams. The line should be 3½" (9 cm) long. Stitch on the marked line through all layers, keeping the seam allowances on both sides turned open. Trim away

the triangle ¼" (6 mm) from the stitching line. Repeat for the other corner.

13 To make the lining, repeat steps 11 and 12 with the other two body pieces, leaving an 8" (20.5 cm) opening along one side.

14 Turn the outer bag right side out. Pin the lid to the center back upper edge of the outer bag, right sides together. Pin the ends of the webbing handle to the right side upper edge of the outer bag over the side seams.

15 With the outer bag right side out and the lining inside out, slip the outer bag into the lining and pin the two together along the upper edge, sandwiching the lid and handle between them. Stitch.

16 Turn the bag right side out through the opening in the lining. Stitch the opening closed. Topstitch the upper edge of the bag. Adhere the monogram to the bag front.

DELUXE
LINEN NAPKINS

MATERIALS

(For one napkin)

Paper and pencil for drawing pattern

Carpenter's square or T-square ruler

⅝ yd (0.6 m) linen, natural color

⅜ yd (0.35 m) linen, bright color

Fabric marking pen or pencil

Thread

Hand-sewing needle, optional

Why match when you can mix? Each dinner napkin in this set has a different colored border. Choose natural-colored linen for the napkin and coordinating jewel tones for the generous borders. You can, of course, make a matched set instead, or supersize the instructions and make a bordered tablecloth. Give a set to your host, to a bride and groom, or to anyone who loves to set a beautiful table.

FINISHED SIZE: 18" (46 CM) SQUARE.

RETRO KITCHEN PLACEMATS AND NAPKINS

As bright and cheerful as a fifties kitchen, these placemats are a fun gift for a busy family because they are tough and wipe clean. Oilcloth placemats are great for outdoor dining, too. The only sewing is one row bordering the scalloped edges. Use two different fabrics so the placemats are reversible. You can use the same pattern to make coordinating cotton napkins.

MATERIALS

(For two placemats and two napkins)

Paper and pencil for drawing pattern

Two pieces tissue paper

Carpenter's square or T-square ruler

⅜ yd. (0.35 m) each of two oilcloth coordinates

Thread

⅜ yd. (0.35 m) each of two cotton fabrics

Fabric marking pen or pencil

Hand-sewing needle

1. Enlarge the pattern on page 94, and cut it out. Cut a rectangle of tissue paper 14" × 20" (35.5 × 51 cm). Fold the tissue paper in half lengthwise and crosswise. Unfold it and trace the outline of the pattern in each quadrant. Mark a stitching line ¼" (6 mm) inside the outline. Repeat for each placemat.

2. Cut two rectangles of oilcloth 14" × 20" (35.5 × 51 cm). Place them wrong sides together, and pin the tissue paper pattern over the top, pinning only into the area outside the scalloped line. (Pins will leave holes, so avoid pinning within the body of the placemat.) With the tissue paper facing up, stitch on the stitching line all around the placemat.

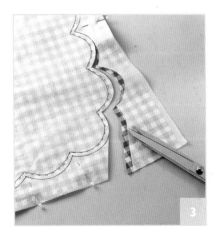

3. Carefully cut through all layers along the pattern outline. Tear away the tissue paper.

4. For napkins, cut 14" × 20" (35.5 × 51 cm) rectangles from two coordi-

nating fabrics. Trace the pattern on one fabric, and cut it out. Pin the fabrics right sides together and stitch the ¼" (6 mm) seam, leaving an opening two scallops long.

5. Trim away the fabrics ⅛" (3 mm) from the stitching line; leave a wider allowance in the area of the opening.

6. Turn the napkin right side out and slipstitch the opening closed.

FINISHED SIZE: 12" × 18" (30.5 × 46 CM)

AUTUMN LEAVES RUNNER

The leaves are falling on this luxurious faux suede table runner. Give it in autumn when someone is decorating for the season. It would be a perfect present for the host of Thanksgiving dinner. Imitation suede is not only fabulous, but easy for sewers since the edges can be left raw. The material is washable, too.

MATERIALS

½ yd. (0.5 m) imitation suede for runner

Carpenter's square or T-square ruler

Fabric marking pen or pencil

Paper and pencil for drawing pattern

¼ yd. (0.25 m) imitation suede in each of three colors for leaves

All-purpose thread in three colors to contrast with leaves

1 Mark a rectangle 15" × 50" (38 × 127 cm) on the imitation suede, using a carpenter's square or T-square ruler and a fabric marking pen or pencil. Cut out the rectangle. Mark the center of one short end; mark points 7½" (19.3 cm) from the end on the long edges. Using a straightedge, draw diagonal lines between the center mark and the side marks. Cut along the marked lines to shape the pointed end. Use the first end to cut the same shape at the other end.

2 Trace the leaf patterns on page 95, and cut them out. Assign a leaf type for each color of contrasting fabric. Trace each leaf eight times on the fabric, some the mirror image of others. Cut them out.

3 Using a fabric marking pen or pencil, draw vein lines on each leaf. Arrange the leaves randomly along the outer edges of the runner, keeping them at least ½" (1.3 cm) from the runner's edge and overlapping them only slightly if necessary.

4 Set the sewing machine for a zigzag stitch of medium width and short length. Satin stitch along the vein lines of each leaf, extending the center vein below the leaf to make a stem.

DESIGNER'S TIP

It is important to choose an imitation suede, such as Ultrasuede, that won't ravel on the cut edges.

FINISHED SIZE: 15" × 50" (38 × 127 CM)

BEADED TABLE SCARF

A table scarf is an elegant gift for someone who loves to decorate and entertain. The style today is to curve and scrunch up a table runner down the middle of a table or buffet, then add candlesticks or other table decorations along the sides. The reverse is a different color, and the contrast is lovely. Select a beautifully embroidered, beaded, or lace fabric and a coordinating plain silk. Add posh bead fringe trim to the scarf ends, and in minutes you've created a masterpiece.

MATERIALS

2 yd. (1.85 m) embellished fabric
Carpenter's square or T-square ruler
Fabric marking pen or pencil
2 yd. (1.85 m) plain silk fabric
7/8 yd. (0.8 m) bead fringe trim
Thread
Hand-sewing needle

1 Mark a rectangle 16" × 71" (40.5 × 180.5 cm) on the wrong side of the embellished fabric, using a carpenter's square or T-square ruler and a fabric marking pen or pencil. Cut out the rectangle. Use this piece to cut a matching piece of the plain silk. Dimensions include 1/2" (1.3 cm) seam allowances.

2 Examine the fabric carefully for beads or sequins that may be along the seam lines. Snip away these embellishments without compromising the fabric to avoid breaking a needle while sewing.

3 Cut two lengths of bead fringe trim, each 15" (38 cm) long. Pin the heading of one trim piece to one short end of the scarf on the right side with the beads facing inward. The inner edge of the heading should be 1/2" (1.3 cm)

from the edge. Baste the heading to the seam line. Repeat for the other end of the scarf.

4 Pin the plain fabric to the embellished fabric, right sides together, sandwiching the trim between them. Attach a zipper foot to the sewing machine. Stitch 1/2" (1.3 cm) seam around the entire scarf, leaving a 10" (25.5 cm) opening on one side. On the short ends, stitch slowly and carefully, taking care not to stitch into a bead.

5 Trim the seam allowances at the corners diagonally. Turn the scarf right side out and press carefully. Slipstitch the opening closed.

FINISHED SIZE: 15" × 70" (38 × 178 CM)

1 Trace the ornament and desired appliqué patterns on page 96. The ornament pattern includes ¼" (6 mm) seam allowances.

2 Cut two ornaments from fabric and one from interfacing. Trim the seam allowances from the interfacing and fuse it to the wrong side of one ornament piece.

3 Cut pieces of paper-backed fusible web a little larger than each of the appliqué pieces. Fuse them to the wrong side of each appliqué fabric. Trace the appliqué patterns onto the paper backing. Cut out the appliqués, and remove the paper backing.

4 Arrange the appliqués on the right side of the interfaced ornament piece, following the numbered sequence. Fuse them into place.

5 Set the sewing machine for a zigzag stitch with a medium width and very short length. Satin stitch along all cut edges of the appliqué pieces, following the numbered sequence.

6 Hand-stitch embellishments, following the photograph on page 71.

7 Pin the piping around the edge of the ornament, aligning the cut edges, beginning and ending along one straight edge. Clip into the piping seam allowance at the corners to allow it to spread and turn the corner smoothly. Attach a zipper foot to the sewing machine. Baste, beginning a short distance from one end and stopping before you reach the beginning end again. The ends will overlap.

8 Cut one end of the piping straight across. Cut the other end so that it overlaps the first by about 2" (5 cm). Remove 2½" (6.5 cm) of the basting in the long end, exposing the filler cord. Trim the exposed cord so that it butts up against the trimmed and covered end of the cord. Wrap the fabric over both cord ends, turning under

the raw edge to finish. Pin in place and finish basting the piping to the ornament.

9 Cut two lengths of each of the narrow ribbons, each 9" (23 cm) long, and stitch the cut ends to the right side of the ornament.

10 Pin the ornament front to the back, right sides together. Using a zipper foot, stitch just inside the basting line. Leave a short opening along one straight edge.

11 Turn the ornament right side out and slipstitch the opening closed.

12 Cut a 4" (10 cm) length of narrow ribbon and slip it through the hole in a paper tag. Stitch the ribbon ends to the back of the ornament at the bottom point. Write the date and greeting on the tag.

DESIGNER'S TIP

Fat quarters purchased at a quilt shop are great for the ornaments and appliqués. These pre-cut pieces measure 18" × 22" (46 × 56 cm), so there is less waste and they are often arranged in coordinating groups.

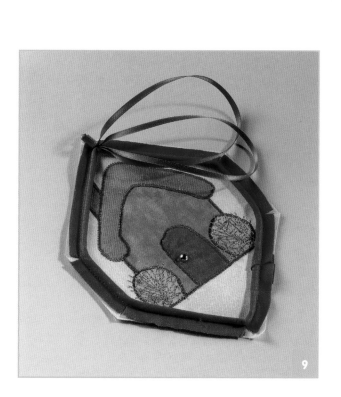

SHEER GIFT BAGS

Present a gift in a sheer bag you made yourself. Sheer fabric that is crisp and firmly woven, such as organdy, works best because it will hold its shape. Directions are given for three different sizes: a tall bag, which is especially useful for a bottle of wine; a medium size bag, perfect for a pillar candle; and a small bag that might hold a gift of jewelry.

FINISHED SIZES:

TALL BAG 4" WIDE × 14" TALL (10 × 35.5 CM)

MEDIUM BAG 6" WIDE × 11" TALL (15 × 28 CM)

SMALL BAG 3" WIDE × 5" TALL (7.5 × 12.7 CM)

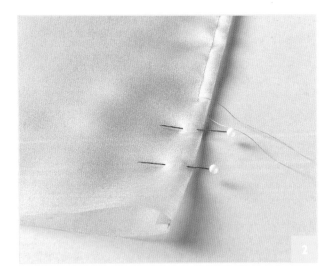

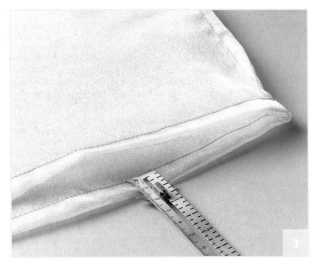

1 Using paper, pencil, and a carpenter's square or T-square ruler, draw a pattern for the size bag you want to make:

Tall bag: 17" wide × 18" tall (43 × 46 cm)

Medium bag: 25" wide × 15" tall (63.5 × 38 cm)

Small bag: 13" wide × 10" tall (33 × 25.5 cm)

2 Cut one piece of sheer fabric, using the pattern. Sew the sides in a French seam as follows: Fold the fabric in half lengthwise, wrong sides together. Stitch a scant 1/4" (6 mm) from the edges. Press the seam open; then turn the bag wrong side out and fold it on the stitching line. Stitch again 1/4" (6 mm) from the stitched edge, encasing the raw edges.

3 Stitch the bottom edges together in a plain 1/4" (6 mm) seam. Turn under the upper edge 1" (2.5 cm) and press. Tuck the cut edge in to meet the crease and pin a 1/2" (1.3 cm) double-fold hem. Stitch along the inner fold.

4 To create a paper-bag bottom for the bag, fold the lower corner, aligning the bottom seam over the side seam. Measure along the bottom seam 2" 5 cm) from the point, for the tall bag; 3" (7.5 cm) from the point for the medium bag; or 1 1/2" (3.8 cm) from the point for the small bag, and draw a line perpendicular to the seams. The line should be 4" (10 cm) long for the tall bag, 6" (15 cm) long for the medium bag, or 3" (7.5 cm) long for the small bag. Stitch on the marked line through all layers. Trim away the triangle 1/4" (6 mm) from the stitching line. Repeat for other corner, centering the bottom seam in the stitching line.

5 Turn the bag right side out. Divide the upper edge into four equal sections, with the seam in the center of one section. Fold the bag from one mark to the bottom corner, and pin. Topstitch 1/4" (6 mm) from the fold, stopping and backstitching 1/4" (6 mm) from the bottom corner. Repeat for the other three sides of the bag.

6 Fold, pin, and stitch a crease in each edge at the base of the bag, starting and stopping with backstitches at the ends of the previous stitching lines.

7 Insert your gift. Tie the top closed with a ribbon and add a gift tag.

DESIGNER'S TIP

No ribbon handy? Just cut a narrow strip of the fabric itself.

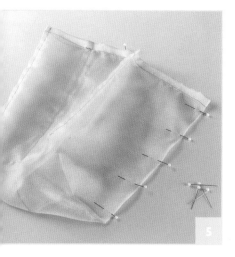

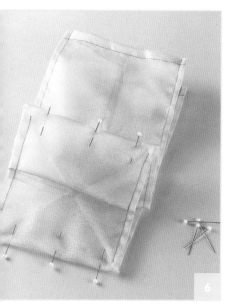

FANCY FABRIC BOXES

MATERIALS

(Amounts vary with box size)

Square or rectangular cardboard box with a lid

Paper and pencil for drawing pattern

Carpenter's square or T-square ruler

Medium-weight woven cotton fabric for box lid, box bottom, and lining

Paper-backed fusible web, 18" (46 cm) wide

Quilt batting

Felt

Glue

Narrow trim or ribbon

Cover boxes with fabric to create decorative storage boxes. Who doesn't need more places to store things? Choose fun, interesting fabric appropriate for the receiver. Place another gift hidden inside, and the presentation becomes two gifts in one.

1 Take the box lid off the box bottom. Measure the width and length of the box lid and box-floor. Measure the height of the box lid and box sides.

2 Draw four rectangular patterns using the following dimensions:

Outer box lid: width equals width of lid plus two times the lid height plus 2" (5 cm); length equals the length of the lid plus two times the lid height plus 2" (5 cm)

Box lid lining: width equals width of lid plus two times the lid height minus 1" (2.5 cm); length equals the length of the lid plus two times the lid height minus 1" (2.5 cm)

Outer box: width equals the width of the box plus two times the box height plus 4" (10 cm); length equals the length of the box plus two times the box height plus 4" (10 cm)

Box lining: width equals width of box plus two times box height minus 2" (5 cm); length equals length of box plus two times box height minus 2" (5 cm)

3 Cut one rectangle each from fabric and paper-backed fusible web a few inches larger than the lid pattern dimensions. Following the web manufacturer's instructions, fuse the web to the wrong side of the fabric. Do not remove paper. Trace the lid pattern on the paper backing, and cut it out. Remove the paper backing.

4 Repeat step 3 for the lid lining, outer box, and box lining. Cut a piece of quilt batting to fit the top of the lid. Cut a piece of felt to fit the bottom of the box.

5 Place the lid fabric, adhesive side up, on the work surface. Center the quilt batting on the outside of the box lid, and turn it facedown over the center of the fabric. Wrap the fabric around the outside of the box lid, pulling the sides of the fabric up the sides of the lid with cut edges even. Pin the fabric at the corners and trim, leaving ½" (1.3 cm) of fabric beyond the pin.

6 Fuse the fabric to the lid sides. At each corner, wrap excess fabric from the side around the corner and fuse it to the lid end. Then fold under excess fabric from the lid end even with the edge and finish fusing the fabric to the lid end.

7 Wrap extra fabric to the inside of the lid and fuse in place.

8 Center the lining inside the lid. Fuse the center first, then fuse the sides. Trim corners and tuck in excess fabric as necessary.

9 Fuse the outer-box fabric and lining to the box bottom, as in steps 5 to 8, disregarding the quilt batting.

10 Glue felt to the bottom of the box. Glue ribbon around the lower edge of the box lid.

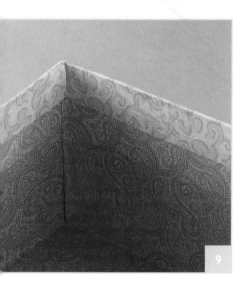

DESIGNER'S TIP

This no-sew project is a breeze when you use paper-backed fusible web and your steam iron. The web is easy to work with and it eliminates the need for messy glue.

PATTERNS

Silk Beauty Bag
(enlarge 200%)

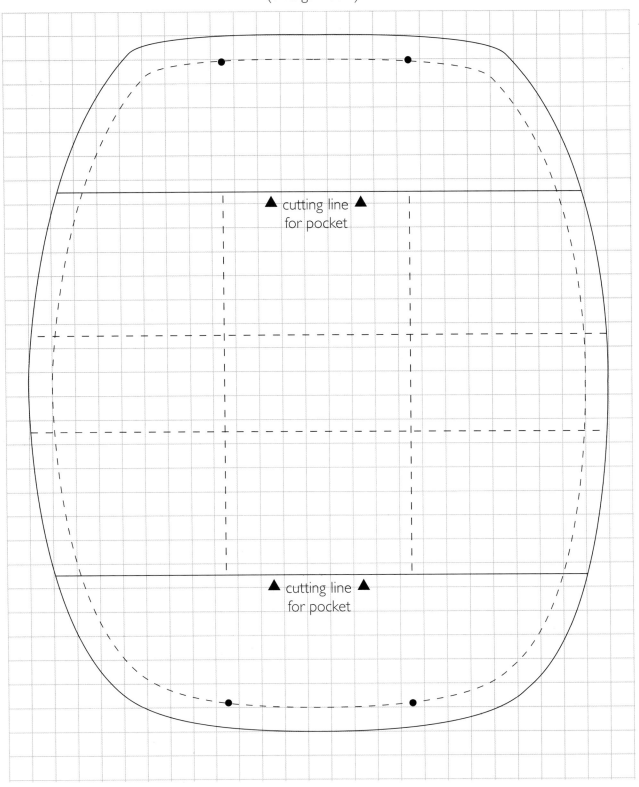

▲ cutting line ▲
for pocket

▲ cutting line ▲
for pocket

1 square = ½" (1.3 cm)

Beach Babe Tote
(enlarge 200%)

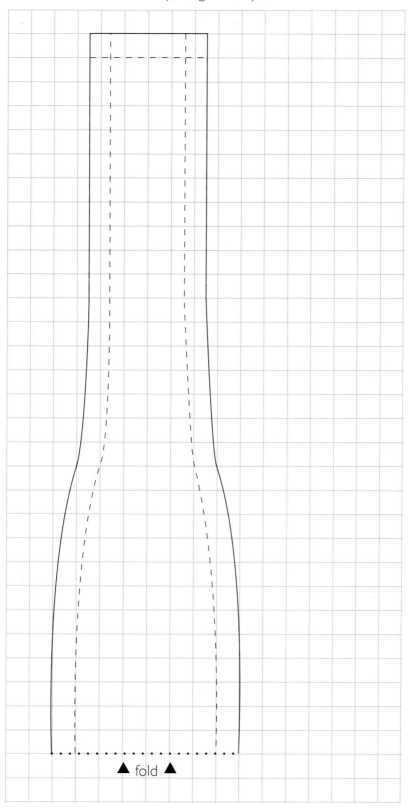

▲ fold ▲

1 square = ½" (1.3 cm)

Stadium Cushion Soccer Ball (full size)

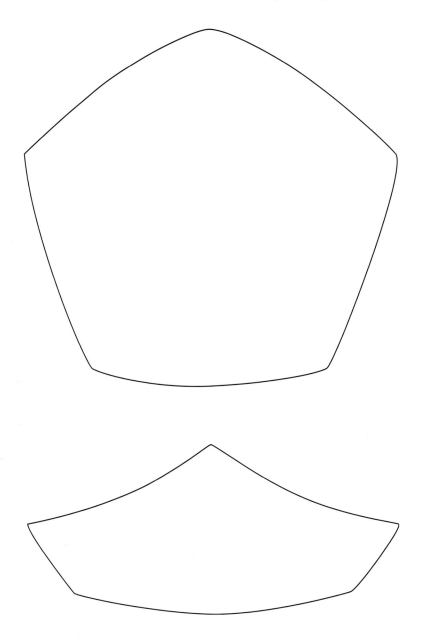

Stadium Cushion Baseball
(enlarge 200%)

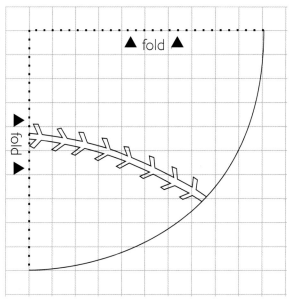

▲ fold ▲

fold

I square = ½" (1.3 cm)

Stadium Cushion Football
(enlarge 200%)

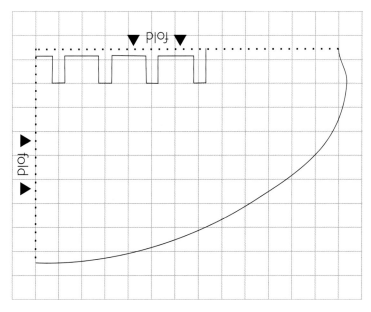

▼ fold ▼

fold

I square = ½" (1.3 cm)

Stadium Cushion Basketball
(enlarge 200%)

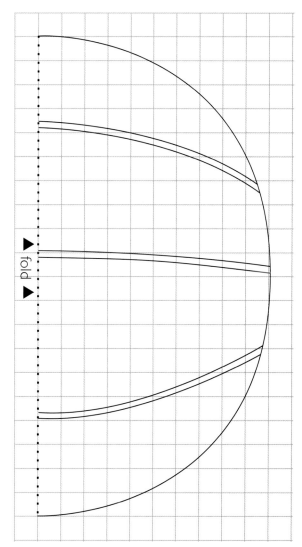

fold

I square = ½" (1.3 cm)

Custom Necktie Front
(enlarge 200%)

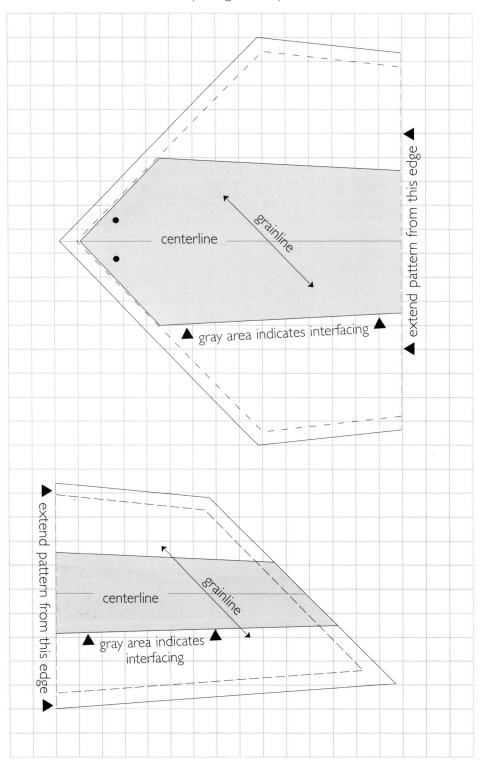

centerline

grainline

gray area indicates interfacing

extend pattern from this edge

centerline

grainline

gray area indicates interfacing

extend pattern from this edge

1 square = ½" (1.3 cm)

Custom Necktie Back
(enlarge 200%)

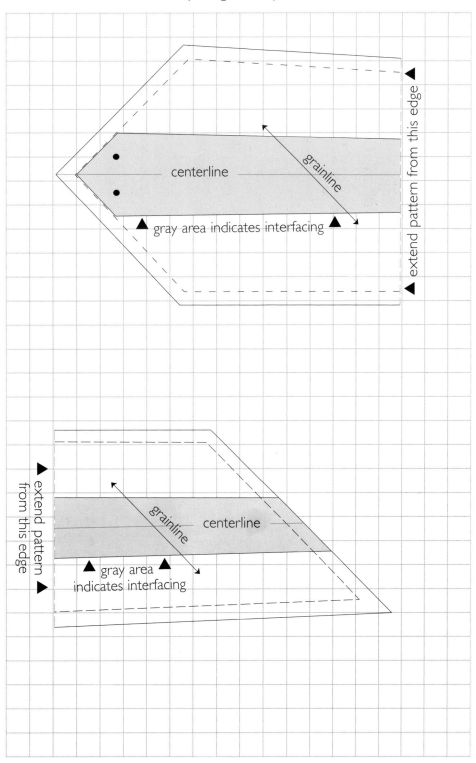

centerline

grainline

gray area indicates interfacing

extend pattern from this edge

grainline

centerline

gray area
indicates interfacing

extend pattern
from this edge

1 square = ½" (1.3 cm)

Custom Necktie Lining
(enlarge 200%)

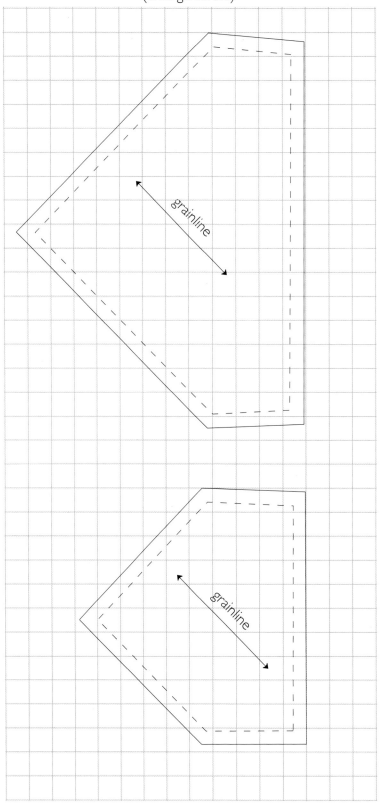

grainline

grainline

I square = 1/2" (1.3 cm)

Friendly Elephant Bib Head
(enlarge 133%)

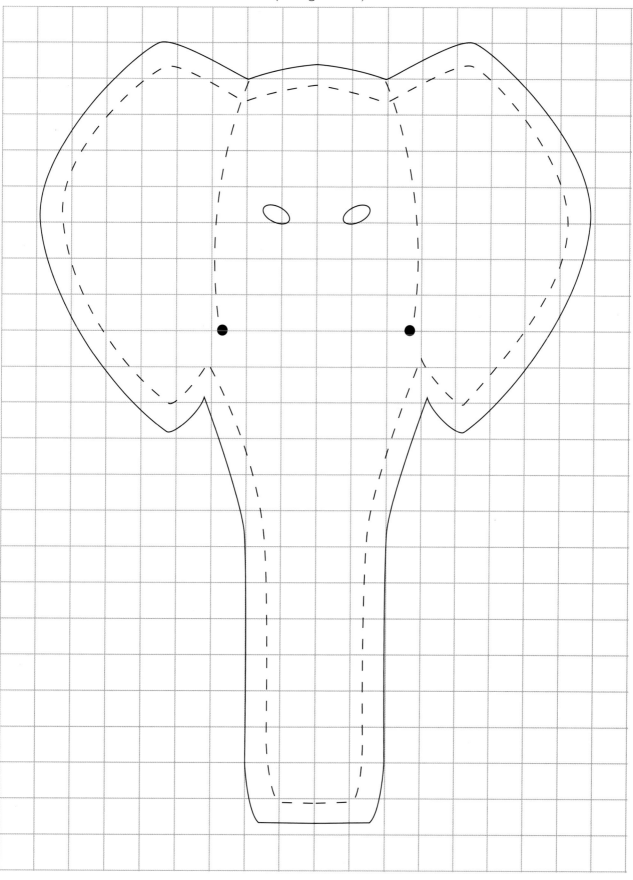

1 square = ½" (1.3 cm)

Friendly Elephant Bib (enlarge 133%)

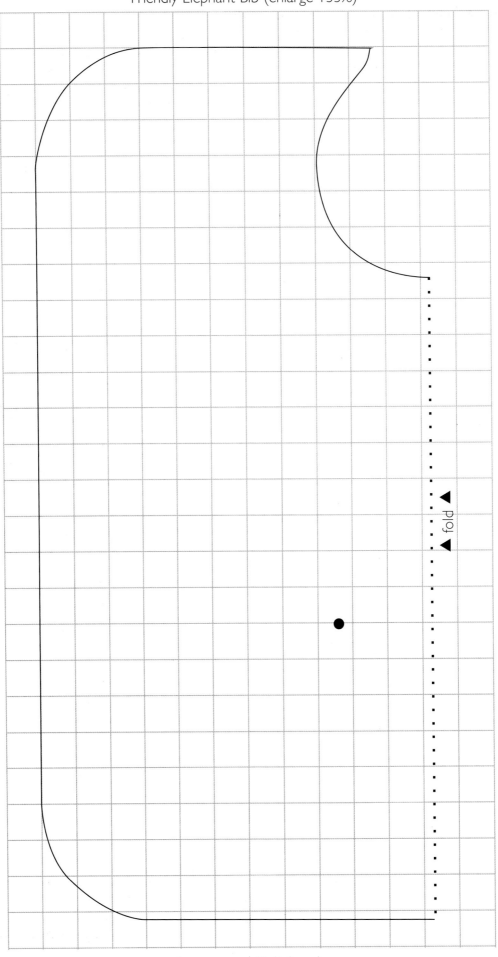

fold ◄
◄

I square = ½" (1.3 cm)

Friendly Elephant Mouth & Tongue (enlarge 133%)

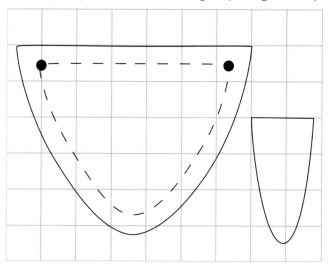

Curly Soft Bear (enlarge 200%)

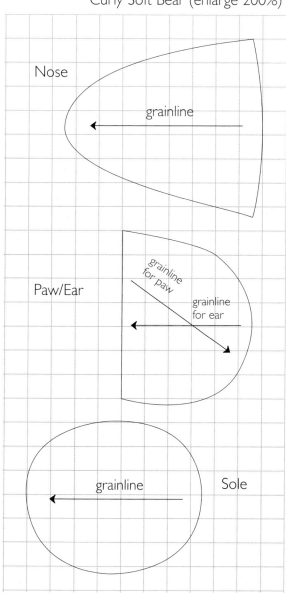

Nose

grainline

Paw/Ear

grainline
for paw

grainline
for ear

grainline

Sole

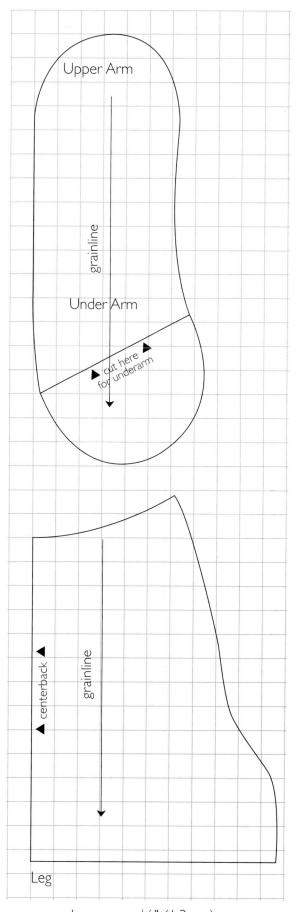

Upper Arm

grainline

Under Arm

cut here
for underarm

centerback

grainline

Leg

1 square = ½" (1.3 cm)

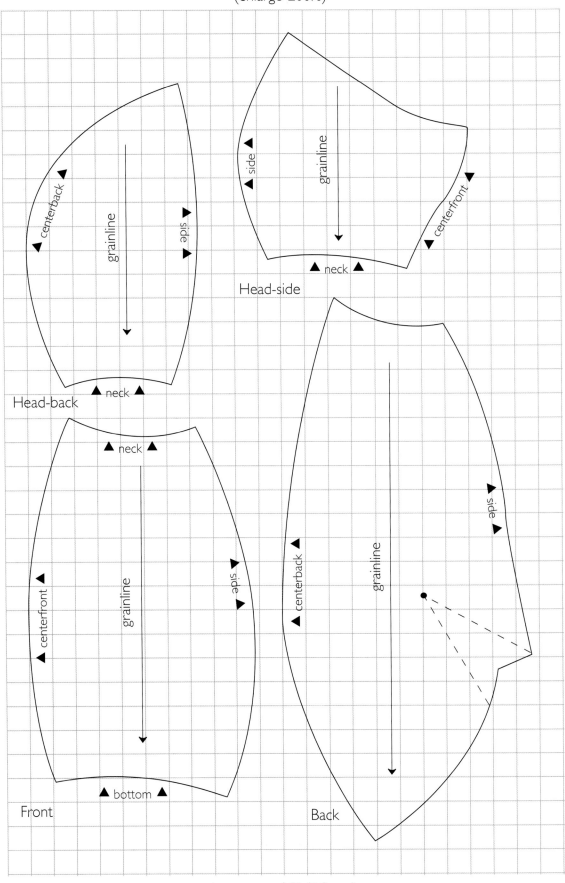

Head-side

Head-back

neck

Front

bottom

Back

side

centerback

grainline

centerfront

1 square = 1/2" (1.3 cm)

Puppy-Dog Hat
(enlarge 133%)

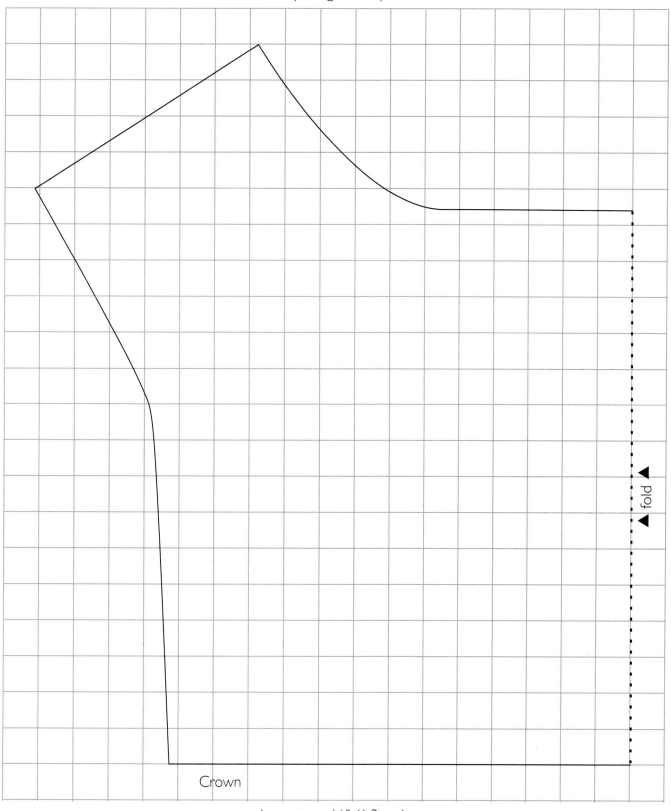

Crown

fold

1 square = ½" (1.3 cm)

My Own Lunch Bag
(enlarge 200%)

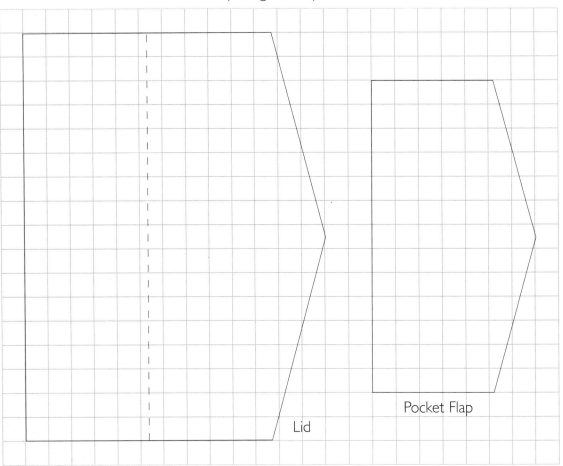

Lid

Pocket Flap

Retro Kitchen Placemat
(enlarge 200%)

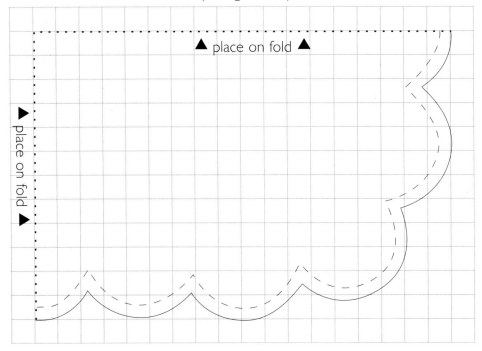

▲ place on fold ▲

◄ place on fold ►

1 square = 1/2" (1.3 cm)

Autumn Leaves Table Runner
(full size)

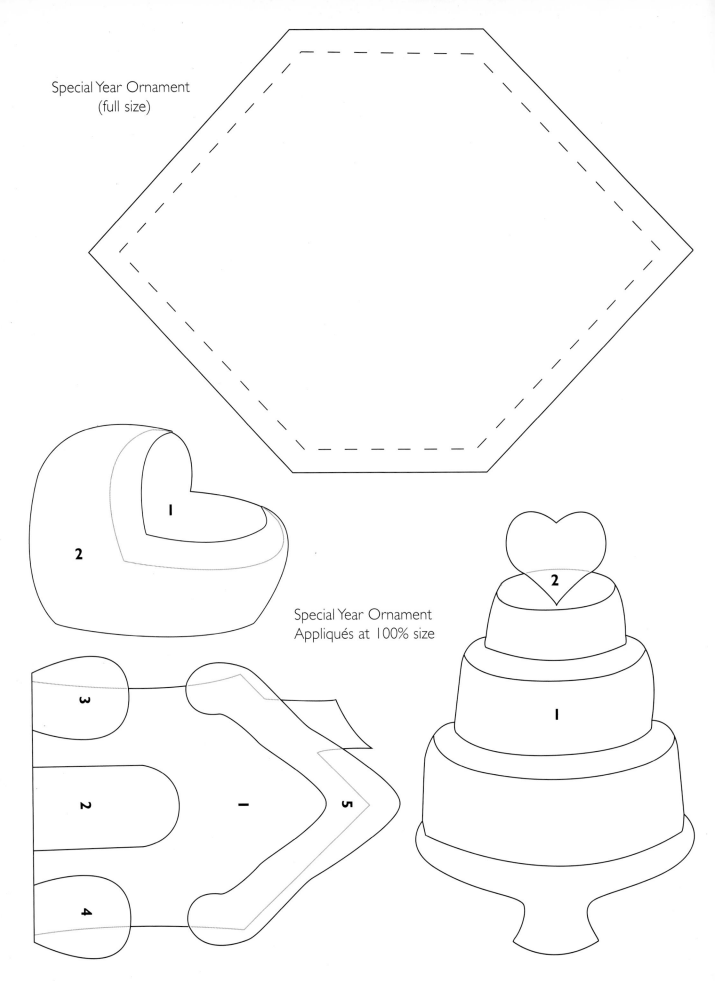

Special Year Ornament
(full size)

Special Year Ornament
Appliqués at 100% size